GREETINGS
CARDS

masterclass

LIANNE SOUTH & ROSALIND BECKMAN

AN INSPIRATIONAL GUIDE WITH FOURTEEN STYLISH PROJECTS

First published in 2000 by
Design Eye Publishing Limited,
4-6 Dunmow Road, Bishop's Stortford,
Hertfordshire CM23 5HL, United Kingdom.

Projects and styling by Lianne South
Text by Rosalind Beckman
Design by Venita Kidwai/Diane Hand
Edited by Raje Airey
Photography by Chris Linton
Step illustrations by Maxine Hamil

© 2000 Design Eye Holdings Limited

ISBN 1 84026 129 3

1 3 5 7 9 10 8 6 4 2

Manufactured in China

CONTENTS

CHAPTER ONE

Introduction

The origin of greetings cards can be traced back to Ancient Egypt, when written messages accompanied New Year gifts. However, greetings cards as we know them, first became popular during the nineteenth century. Their popularity increased enormously in the early twentieth century with the evolution of a cheap and efficient postal system.

Today greetings cards are available in an infinite variety of designs to match almost any mood. Many people like the personal touch of sending a handmade greetings card, making birthdays and other celebrations into even more of an occasion. This book describes some of the methods and gives practical projects for making your own cards. The Introduction gives you helpful advice on which materials to use and describes some useful techniques, such as collage and stencilling. It also contains easy-to-follow instructions on how to make your own paper.

EQUIPMENT AND
Materials

G reetings cards are inexpensive to make. Your Masterclass contains a set of templates and a variety of materials to get you started – including coloured card, fabric, wire, paint, coloured threads, and a mould and deckle for making paper. You'll also need tracing paper, scissors and glue.

PAPER

Your Masterclass contains green and blue card to get you started, but paper is available in a wide variety of colours, weight and textures. Most machine-made papers are uncoated and they are available in a range of plain and textured finishes. Coated papers have highly smooth surfaces on one or both sides and are available in gloss or dull finishes. Handmade papers are made from cotton or linen rags, and speciality papers include tissue, crêpe, tracing and corrugated card. For special effects, it is worth experimenting with making your own paper (see page 12).

PAINTS

Water-based paints are used for the projects in this book as they dry quickly. Your Masterclass comes with a special stencil paint in silver. Gouache paints and the cheaper poster paints both cover a surface well and come in bright colours. Acrylic paints also come in a wide range of colours. They are fast-drying, waterproof, and are less likely to crack with age. Acrylic paints can be thinned with water to give a less intense colour. If you prefer a more subtle finish, use watercolours, which are sold in pans or in tubes.

INKS

Inks can be waterproof or non-waterproof. Use waterproof ink if you want to apply a wash or tint on top of a line drawing, otherwise the line work will run. These inks dry to a slightly glossy finish.

Non-waterproof inks are used for laying washes over waterproof ink drawings. They can be mixed with distilled water to produce a range of lighter tones and they dry to a matt finish.

FABRICS

A collection of assorted fabrics is useful for making collages. Your Masterclass contains enough fabric pieces to make the Fabric Collage project on page 34, but it is also worth building up your own collection of fabric scraps. One of the best sources for material is a dressmaker, or try hunting through the bargain boxes in department stores.

OTHER MATERIALS

Try using unusual materials to give your cards a distinctive feel. Your Masterclass contains copper, silver and brass wires which are used in the Twisted Wire project on page 24. It's also a good idea to build up a stock of trimmings, coloured threads and silks, and other bits and pieces, which can be used to give that extra special finishing touch!

Techniques

It is relatively easy to make greetings cards without any special technical skill – the artistic effect is created by the choice of colours, materials and overall composition. However there are a few simple tips and techniques which are useful useful to know.

COLLAGE

The word collage comes from the French word meaning 'to gum' and refers to the technique of creating a picture in two dimensions or low relief by gluing paper, fabric or other decorative items onto a background. Depending on the effect you wish to create, you can produce a traditional scene or an abstract image. Photomontage, the construction of a picture from parts of different photographs, is a modern form of collage and can be used to create an interesting and dynamic effect.

USING GLUES

Most greetings cards require some form of adhesive. Always allow sufficient time for glue to dry before carrying on with the rest of the project. Glue sticks and glue pens are ideal for light gluing, especially when you want to control the amount of glue you want to use, while PVA glue is a good quick-bonding, all-purpose glue. Spray adhesive is convenient but should be used in a well-ventilated area and kept safely out of the reach of children. Double-sided tape can be used in place of glue. Use masking tape when you want to keep something in position temporarily while you work.

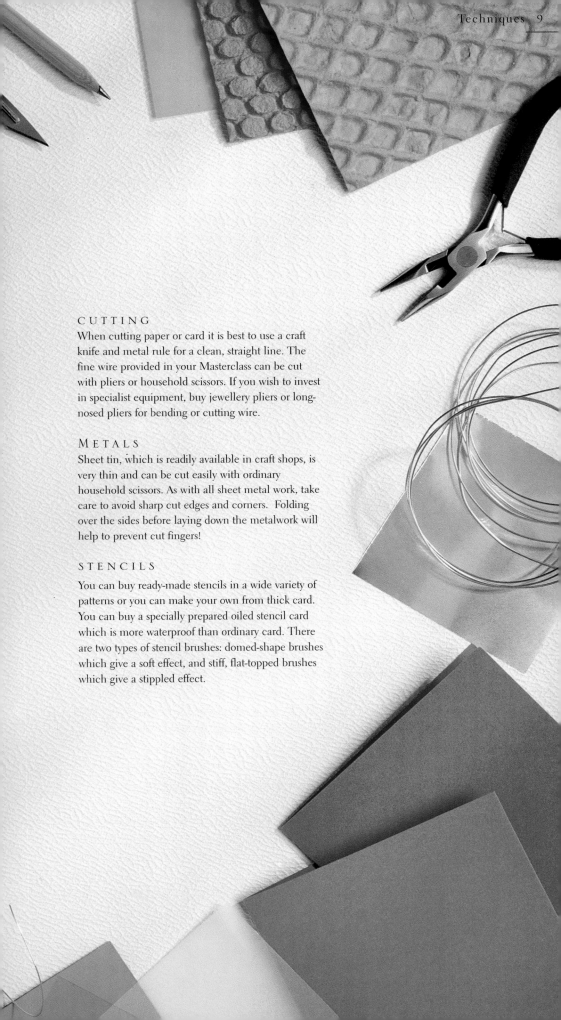

CUTTING

When cutting paper or card it is best to use a craft
knife and metal rule for a clean, straight line. The
fine wire provided in your Masterclass can be cut
with pliers or household scissors. If you wish to invest
in specialist equipment, buy jewellery pliers or long-
nosed pliers for bending or cutting wire.

METALS

Sheet tin, which is readily available in craft shops, is
very thin and can be cut easily with ordinary
household scissors. As with all sheet metal work, take
care to avoid sharp cut edges and corners. Folding
over the sides before laying down the metalwork will
help to prevent cut fingers!

STENCILS

You can buy ready-made stencils in a wide variety of
patterns or you can make your own from thick card.
You can buy a specially prepared oiled stencil card
which is more waterproof than ordinary card. There
are two types of stencil brushes: domed-shape brushes
which give a soft effect, and stiff, flat-topped brushes
which give a stippled effect.

Some of the projects require you to prepare materials in advance. However, if you follow the instructions below, you will easily be able to complete the more complicated projects that appear later in the book.

PRESSING LEAVES AND FLOWERS

The best time to pick flowers and leaves for pressing is in the morning when the sun has caused the dew to evaporate but before there is any danger of wilting. If you are unable to press them straight away, place the stems in just enough water to keep them fresh.

Whether you use a flower press or a pile of heavy books, you will need a large quantity of blotting paper. Place the flowers on the blotting paper, making sure that each piece has enough room to spread under the weight of the press or books. If possible, leave a 2.5 cm (1 in) gap around the edges so that all the pieces are pressed consistently.

Unless they vary greatly in thickness, press the leaves, stems and flowers together. Flowers such as pansies can be divided into individual petals before pressing. Leave the flowers in the press for at least a week before using so that they are thoroughly dry.

DRYING FRUIT

Most fruits dry well. Choose fruit which is ripe but firm and unblemished. When drying, pieces of fruit should not touch each other and all cut fruit should be dried cut-side up at first.

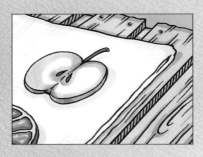

Place the fruit on slatted wooden trays (wooden fruit boxes are perfect for this) lined with a double layer of muslin or viscose cloth. You need a steady temperature between 50–60°C (120–140°F) and a place where warm air can circulate freely. A warm airing cupboard or an oven set to its lowest possible setting are good places. Buy a thermometer to check that the temperature is kept constant.

When completely dry, apple rings will look leathery, soft fruit should yield no juice when you cut into it and bananas will have a wavy edge. Cool the fruit thoroughly before packing into paper bags or cardboard cartons. Store in a cool, dry place.

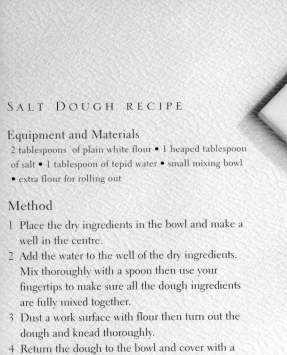

SALT DOUGH RECIPE

Equipment and Materials

2 tablespoons of plain white flour • 1 heaped tablespoon of salt • 1 tablespoon of tepid water • small mixing bowl • extra flour for rolling out

Method

1 Place the dry ingredients in the bowl and make a well in the centre.
2 Add the water to the well of the dry ingredients. Mix thoroughly with a spoon then use your fingertips to make sure all the dough ingredients are fully mixed together.
3 Dust a work surface with flour then turn out the dough and knead thoroughly.
4 Return the dough to the bowl and cover with a plastic bag to keep it airtight. Leave for at least ten minutes before using.
5 Unused dough can be kept in an airtight container to prevent it from drying out.

TYING A FRENCH KNOT

Method

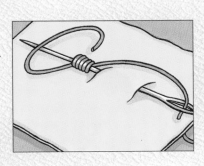

1 Take the needle from the back of the work to the front. Leave a small end hanging.
2 Hold the needle and go into the fabric and out again, as if you were pinning something.
3 Wind the thread around the tip of the needle. Pull the needle through the wound thread to make the knot.
4 Take the needle through to the back of the material and tie the two ends to secure it.

Note: You can vary the size of the knots, depending on how many times you wind the thread round the needle.

HANDMADE
Paper

A mould and deckle is provided with your Masterclass. It is the essential tool for making handmade paper and consists of two identical frames, except the mould is covered with mesh. You will also need some scrap paper, a large shallow bowl, some viscose cloths, two wooden boards and a pile of heavy books.

1 Take some scrap paper in a colour of your choice and tear it up into small squares, about 3.5 cm (1¼ in). You will need enough paper to fill a small bucket. Leave overnight in cold water so that the paper is thoroughly soaked through.

2 Put the wet paper into a liquidiser goblet until it is an eighth to a quarter full. Cover with warm water until the goblet is two-thirds full. Process the paper until it has completely broken down.

3 Fill your bowl with hand-hot water to a depth of 10 cm (4 in) and add the pulped paper. You need to achieve a broth-like consistency. Mix the pulp thoroughly with your hands.

4 Place the deckle on the mould with the netted surface sandwiched in the middle. Slide it down to the bottom of the bowl then bring it back up, pulling it towards you. Shake gently for a few seconds.

5 Use a firm wooden board 10 cm (4 in) wider than your sheets of paper. Cover the board with a damp cloth. Remove the deckle and invert the mould onto the cloth. Lift off the mould. Repeat until you have used all the pulp.

6 Place a wooden board, identical to the first, over the paper and weigh it down with the books. Leave the boards in a container while the excess water is squeezed out.

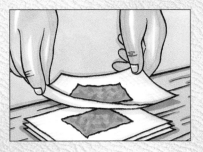

7 After about 30 minutes, take the press from the container and remove the top board. Carefully lift out each cloth with its sheet of paper on it, by holding diagonally opposite corners.

8 Place your sheet with the cloth uppermost on a flat, dry, waterproof surface and carefully peel off the cloth. Use a soft, wide brush to remove any loose surface fibres, then leave it to dry overnight.

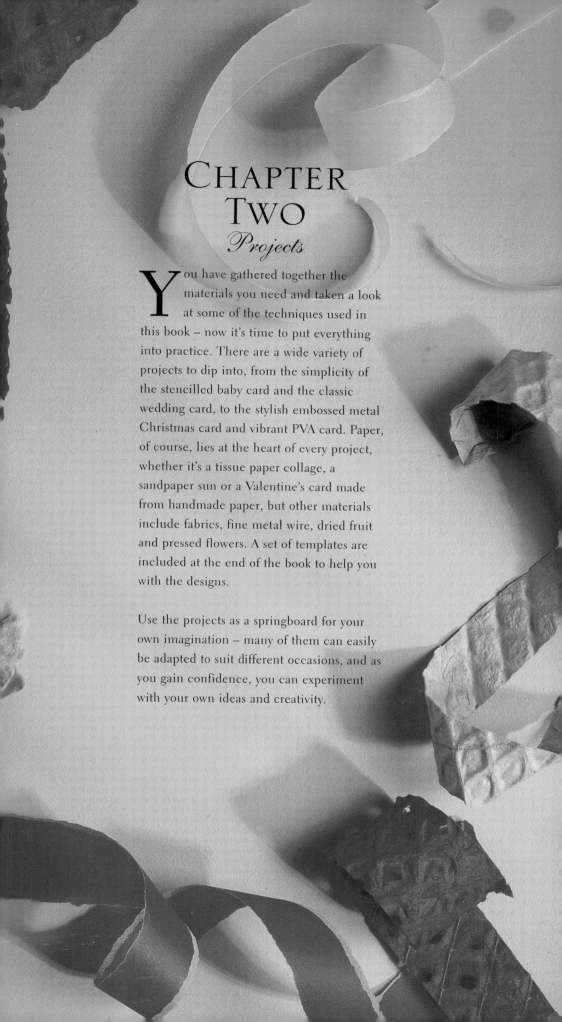

CHAPTER TWO
Projects

You have gathered together the materials you need and taken a look at some of the techniques used in this book – now it's time to put everything into practice. There are a wide variety of projects to dip into, from the simplicity of the stencilled baby card and the classic wedding card, to the stylish embossed metal Christmas card and vibrant PVA card. Paper, of course, lies at the heart of every project, whether it's a tissue paper collage, a sandpaper sun or a Valentine's card made from handmade paper, but other materials include fabrics, fine metal wire, dried fruit and pressed flowers. A set of templates are included at the end of the book to help you with the designs.

Use the projects as a springboard for your own imagination – many of them can easily be adapted to suit different occasions, and as you gain confidence, you can experiment with your own ideas and creativity.

PAPER
Collage

This cheerful Easter card echoes the colours of spring. Layers of brightly-coloured paper are used to make a striking Easter egg collage, in which the sharpness of the green and yellow background are balanced by the softer pink of the egg cup.

Equipment and Materials

lime green greetings card, 110 x 170 mm (4½ x 6½ in) • tissue paper (dark green, lime green, pink, yellow, white) • yellow handmade paper • ruler • glue or spraymount • tracing paper • pencil • template

1   Tear a piece of dark green tissue paper against the edge of a ruler to make a rectangle, approximately 85 x 105 mm (3½ x 4½ in). Stick the tissue paper onto the front of the greetings card.

2   Stick a piece of yellow handmade paper, approximately 65 x 65 mm (2½ x 2½ in), onto the tissue paper. Tear a 40 mm (2 in) square from both the dark green and the lime green tissue paper. Stick these squares onto the yellow paper, overlapping the dark green paper slightly with the lime green paper.

3   Trace the egg and egg cup from the template onto the appropriate tissue paper. Tear them out carefully and stick them into position on the front of the card.

SPIRAL

This card uses the cogs and wheel that come with your Masterclass to draw spiral patterns on the card. The variation in tone and shape adds to the impact of the design. This card uses shades of orange and yellow, but you can experiment with other colours in the same way.

Equipment and Materials

terracotta greetings card 165 x 165 mm (6½ x 6½ in) • yellow, white, ochre and orange paints • watercolour paper • wheel and cogs from your kit • fine black pen • double-sided tape • varnish

1 Using the paints, mix several different shades of yellow. Paint nine areas, 55mm x 55 mm (2¼ x 2¼ in) square, in different yellows on the paper. Leave it to dry.

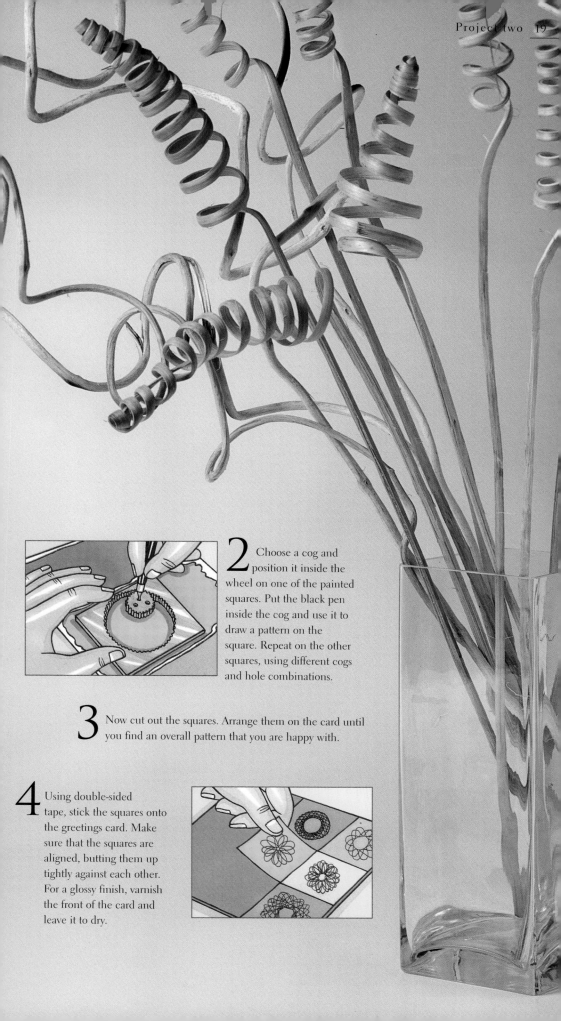

2 Choose a cog and position it inside the wheel on one of the painted squares. Put the black pen inside the cog and use it to draw a pattern on the square. Repeat on the other squares, using different cogs and hole combinations.

3 Now cut out the squares. Arrange them on the card until you find an overall pattern that you are happy with.

4 Using double-sided tape, stick the squares onto the greetings card. Make sure that the squares are aligned, butting them up tightly against each other. For a glossy finish, varnish the front of the card and leave it to dry.

DRIED
Fruit

The dried fruit of this design makes a spectacular autumnal greetings
card. The use of paper and card which both tones and contrasts
with the fruit is highly effective, and using just one piece of fruit gives a
particularly dramatic effect.

Equipment and Materials

dried fruit • natural, green or orange handmade or textured paper • glue • double-sided tape •
spray mount • green and orange greetings card • craft knife • ruler

1 Dry the fruit of your choice following
the method shown on page 10.

2 Experiment with the coloured cards
to find one that looks good with
your fruit. Cut the card according
to the size and shape of your piece
of fruit.

3 Tear or cut a piece of paper or card into a square about 10 mm (4 in) larger than the piece of fruit. Now tear or cut a second piece of paper or card into a square a little larger than the first one. Stick the second piece of paper or card onto the first.

4 Finally, stick the glued paper or card to the front of the greetings card. Finish by gluing the fruit securely onto the front.

TEXTURED
Sandpaper

T his card uses layered sandpaper to make an unusual design, and the different grades of paper give it an interesting textured look. The card is quick to make and the simple collage effect is easy to achieve. For a jazzier effect, use a contrasting colour for the background.

Equipment and Materials

terracotta greetings card 190 x 140 mm (7½ x 5½ in) • four or five sheets of sandpaper in different grades and colours • scissors • double-sided tape • PVA glue • paintbrush • template

1 Take the template and cut one circle for the sun, ten sun rays and the zigzag border in different colours from the sandpaper sheets.

2 Arrange the cut-out pieces of sandpaper on the front of the greetings card and stick them in place with double-sided tape.

3 Using the PVA as if it were paint, carefully paint a swirl on the centre of the sun and zigzags on each of the rays. Leave the greetings card to dry in a warm place.

TWISTED *Wire*

Dip into your Masterclass to make this stylish card. Shades of blue and white handmade paper are used to contrast with the brightness of the wire, while the different twisted shapes add variety and interest to the overall design.

Equipment and Materials

blue greetings card provided, trimmed and folded to 80 x 120 mm (3 x 5 in) • brass, silver and copper wire from your kit • handmade paper in natural and two shades of blue • glue • ruler • double-sided tape • long-nose pliers • craft knife • template

1 Take the blue greetings card from the end of this book and trim it to make a card 80 x 120 mm (3 x 5 in) when folded.

2 From the handmade paper, cut out four squares, approximately 40 x 40 mm (1½ x 1½ in). Next tear out four circles from the paper, small enough to fit inside the squares. Stick one circle onto each square, making sure that the colours contrast well.

3 Using double-sided tape, stick the squares vertically down the centre of the card. Space the squares evenly.

4 Carefully cut out four 2 mm (⅛ in) strips from two of the handmade papers. Stick the strips vertically on either side of the squares to make a border (as in the photograph).

5 Following the outlines on the template, bend the wire into four different shapes. For the flower and star shapes, join the ends by twisting them together. Stick a shape in the centre of each paper circle on the front of your card to complete the design.

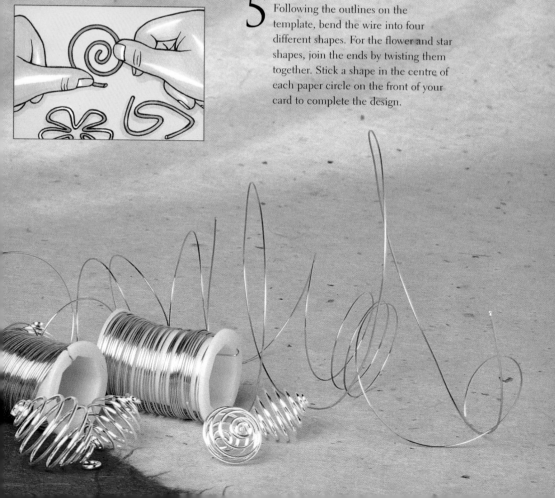

SIMPLE

Stencil

Stencilling is a technique which is easy to master and even the simplest idea can be used to great effect. Here pink is used as the background for a bold nappy pin design to create the perfect card to welcome a new baby.

Equipment and Materials

pale pink greetings card 90 x 140 mm (3½ x 5½ in) • pale pink thin card, 65 x 90 mm (2½ x 3½ in) • pink acrylic paint • corrugated card • paintbrush • thick card • craft knife • pencil • tracing paper • double-sided tape • tracing paper • template

1 Make your nappy pin stencil by tracing the nappy pin from the template and copying it onto a square of thick card. Carefully cut out your new template, using a craft knife.

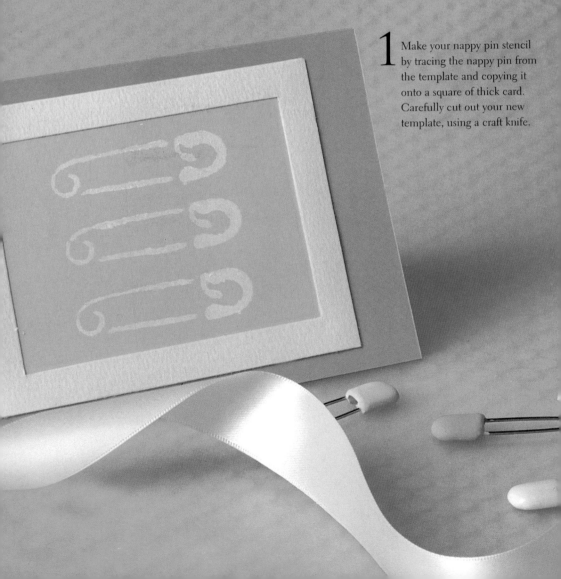

2 Using a sponge, stencil three nappy pins in pink paint into a column onto the piece of thin card. Leave the card to dry.

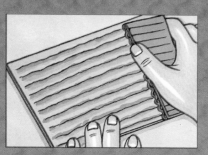

3 Now brush the corrugated card with the pink paint and use it as a stamp to print horizontal lines across the front of the greetings card.

4 Use small pieces of double-sided tape to stick the nappy pins firmly onto the front of the greetings card.

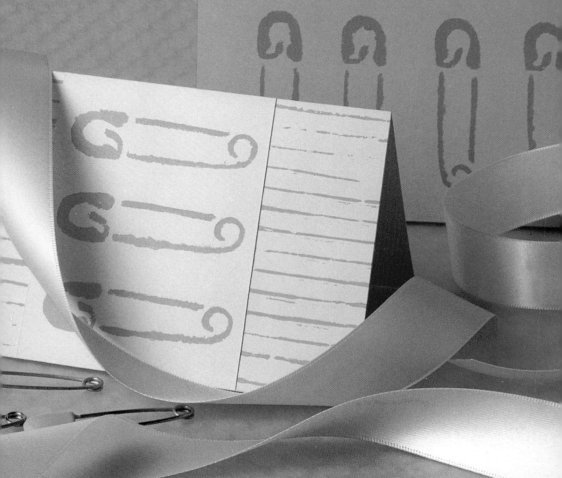

LUXURY
Embossed

T he ultimate in Valentine's cards, this design has hearts and
kisses embossed on handmade paper. The card is created layer
by layer, and the softness of the pink central design harmonises
perfectly with the red border and echoes its pattern.

Equipment and Materials

red greetings card 160 x 110 mm (6½ x 4¼ in) • cream card • lightweight watercolour
paper • mountboard • pencil • cream and pink acrylic paint • craft knife •
paintbrush • double-sided tape • tracing paper • template

1 Trace the hearts and kiss design from the
template and copy onto the mountboard. Cut
the hearts and kiss out, being very careful to
keep the remaining mountboard in one piece.
Trim the edges of the cut-outs so that they are
slightly smaller than the shapes left behind on
the mountboard.

2 Tear a piece of watercolour paper into
a rectangle about 10 mm (½ in) more
all round than the hearts and kiss
design. Soak the paper with water and
lay it on the back of the mountboard
template, pressing it gently into the
shaped holes.

3 Push the cut-out shapes back into their holes, trapping the paper. Leave the shapes to dry in a warm place.

4 Stick the cream card to the red card. Cut a small heart and kiss from the mountboard, using the templates. Use double-sided sticky tape to stick the heart to the wrong end of a pencil. Brush the heart with cream paint and use it to print around the border of the card. Leave a space between the hearts and repeat the process with the kiss shape. Let the border dry.

5 When the embossed watercolour paper design is dry, remove it from the mountboard template. Brush it over with a wash of pink paint and leave it to dry. Finally, stick it in the centre of the greetings card.

AFRICAN
Wax

Taking its inspiration from traditional African designs, this unusual card, which uses a method similar to batik, is a montage of small tiles, each displaying a different pattern. The earthy colours reflect the ethnic designs, which are brought to life by the white background.

Equipment and Materials

white greetings card 95 x 185 mm (3¾ x 7¼ in) • thick white card • sand, terracotta and purple thin card • purple acrylic paint • yellow wax crayon • craft knife • ruler • double-sided tape • PVA glue • template

1 Cut the thick card into eight 40 x 40 mm
(1½ x 1½ in) squares. Using a mixture of
colours, cut eight squares the same size from
the thin card. Use double-sided tape to stick
one thin card square onto each of the thick
square cards.

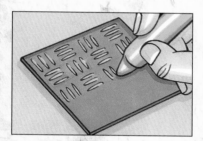

2 Taking one tile at a time and
following the patterns on the
template, copy a design onto
the coloured surface, using
the wax crayon. There is no
need to trace the designs as
freehand work can help to
create the impression of an
authentic ethnic effect.

3 Once each tile has a design on it, paint it
over with a wash of purple acrylic. Make
sure that you paint the sides of the tiles
as well. Wipe away any excess paint with
a tissue. When the paint has dried, coat
each tile with a layer of PVA glue and
leave it to dry once more.

4 Arrange the tiles on the front of the
greetings card in a pleasing pattern,
leaving a 5 mm (¼ in) border and a
5 mm (¼ in) space between each of the
tiles. Secure the tiles to the greetings card
with double-sided tape.

BLOCK
Printing

This dainty card with its pastel colouring and silver print is perfect for a wedding. The design is made using a simple home-made printing block with an old mouse mat for the stamp, but other simple objects, such as corks or pieces of polystyrene could also be used.

Equipment and Materials

silver-grey greetings card 100 x 125 mm (4 x 5 in) • mouse mat • wood off-cut, approximately 65 x 85 mm (2¼ x 3½ in) • silver stencil paint from your kit • duck egg blue acrylic paint • duck egg blue thin card 65 x 85 mm (2¼ x 3½ in) • strong glue • tracing paper • pencil • template

1 Stick the thin blue card in the middle on the front of the greetings card.

2 Trace the patterns from the template onto the mouse mat and carefully cut them out. Stick the shapes onto the wooden block to make a printing stamp.

3 Brush a little silver paint onto the stamp and print the image onto the front of the card.

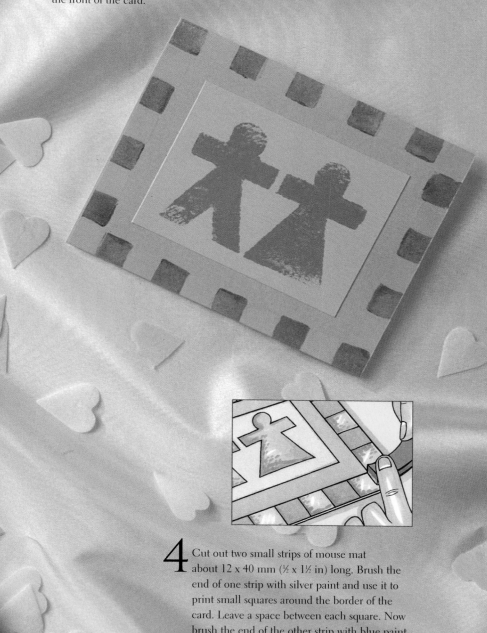

4 Cut out two small strips of mouse mat about 12 x 40 mm (½ x 1½ in) long. Brush the end of one strip with silver paint and use it to print small squares around the border of the card. Leave a space between each square. Now brush the end of the other strip with blue paint and print small squares in the spaces between the silver ones.

FABRIC
Collage

All the materials you need to make this colourful collage are included with your Masterclass. The design is made up of layers of natural fabrics – calico, gingham, hessian and denim – and the traditional effect is completed with some colourful stitching around the outside of the house.

Equipment and Materials

green greetings card provided, folded to 110 x 150mm (4½ x 6 in) • scraps of fabric from your kit • PVA glue • scissors • double-sided tape • needle and coloured thread from your kit • template

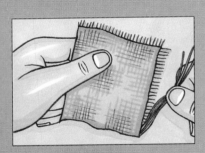

1 Take the green greetings card from the end of this book and trim it to make a card 110 x 150 mm (4½ x 6 in) when folded.

2 Cut out a piece of hessian approximately 75 x 80 mm (3 x 3¼ in). Fray about 5 mm (¼ in) of the material at each edge. Cut out a house, roof and windows from other fabric scraps, using the templates.

3 Glue the house shape in position on the hessian. Repeat this with the roof and then add the windows.

4 Sew some rough stitches around the roof, side walls and door of the house. Sew a cross in each of the windows.

5 Attach the collage to the greetings card with double-sided tape or by using small stitches to keep each corner in place.

SOPHISTICATED
Metal

This stunning card features a Christmas tree pressed into metal, using a simple embossing tool to create the pattern. Although it may look stark in design, the card is full of light and shadow as it reflects the light of its surroundings.

Equipment and Materials

silver greetings card 100 x 170 mm (4 x 6¾ in) • tin sheet • embossing tool (such as an old ball-point pen) • tracing paper • double-sided tape • thin card • ruler • craft knife • scissors • template

1 Trace the Christmas tree design from the template onto tracing paper.

2 Position the tracing paper centrally over the tin sheet and use the embossing tool to trace over the design again, this time pressing firmly into the tin.

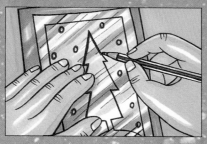

3 Lay the tin sheet onto the card and cut round it, adding an extra 10 mm (½ in) all round.

4 Use double-sided tape to stick the thin card centrally to the wrong side of the tin sheet.

5 Snip the corners off the metal shape and carefully bend over the edges, securing them to the back of the card with double-sided tape. Now stick it to the front of the greetings card.

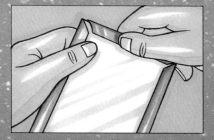

CHINESE
Dough

Chinese calligraphy is a beautiful art form. For this card the letters are formed in an unusual way by scratching the salt dough surface and filling in the impressions with red food colouring. The simplicity of style and colour make this elegant card suitable for all occasions.

Equipment and Materials

cream greetings card 90 x 195 mm (3½ x 7½ in) • salt dough • red food colouring • dark red textured paper • rolling pin • sharp knife • ruler • craft knife • fine paintbrush • glue • spraymount or double-sided tape • template

1 Make up the salt dough following the recipe on page 11. Add a few drops of red food colour to the dough and knead until the colour is even.

2 Use a rolling pin to roll out the dough until it's approximately 3 mm (⅛ in) thick. You may need to flour your surface lightly to prevent the dough from sticking. Using a sharp knife, cut out three rectangles, each approximately 25 x 28 mm (1 x 1¼ in).

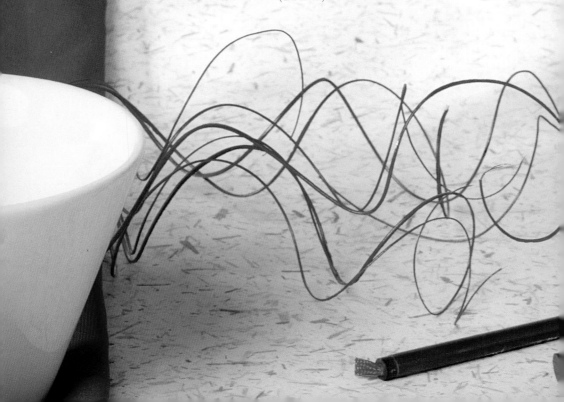

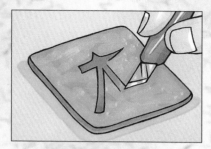

3 With the point of a sharp knife, scratch a Chinese word into the surface of each square, copying those provided on the template. Do this gently so as not to cut right through the dough. Lay the dough rectangles on a baking tray.

4 Dip a paintbrush into the red food colouring and let it drip into the scratched surface of the dough. Drip more colouring until the shape is completely full. Bake at 100°C/gas mark ¼ (200°F) for about 45 minutes. Leave the dough to cool.

5 Cut a long strip of dark red textured paper, about 35 mm (1½ in) wide. Make the strip long enough to wrap over the top and bottom of the card. Use spraymount or double-sided tape to stick the strip to the front of the card about 10 mm (½ in) from the opening edge. Now glue the dough shapes onto the strip. Place one about 10 mm (½ in) from the bottom, then leave a space of about 5 mm (¼ in) between them.

PRESSED
Flowers

This card uses pressed flowers to create a delicate effect. Although the technique is simple, allow time for drying the flowers. According to folklore, flowers have a language of their own. The meaning of pansies – 'tender and pleasant thoughts' – is ideal for a greetings card.

Equipment and Materials

lilac greetings card 120 x 120 mm (5 x 5 in) • eight small pressed flowers • 1 large pressed flower • thin purple card 65 x 65 mm (2½ x 2½ in) • acetate 65 x 65 mm (2½ x 2½ in) • glue • ruler • craft knife • pencil

1 Press the flowers following the instructions on page 10.

2 In the centre of the greetings card, mark out a square about 55 x 55 mm (2¼ x 2¼ in). Opening the card out flat to avoid cutting through the two layers, cut out the square using a craft knife and ruler.

3 Carefully stick the acetate square to the wrong side of the hole to create a window.

4 Stick the small flowers to the front of the card, spacing them equally on the border around the window.

5 Stick the purple card centrally on the inside of the greetings card, so that when the card is closed, the purple lies directly under the acetate window.

6 Finally, stick the large flower in the centre of the purple square. Leave it to dry.

VIBRANT
PVA

The bright colours and bold design give an exciting and contemporary feel to this greetings card. Here paper with a snakeskin look to it has been chosen, but you can use any paper with a well-defined texture. The French knots, added randomly to the card, bring in another interesting element to the design.

Equipment and Materials

orange greetings card 110 x 170 mm (4¼ x 6¾ in) • thick card, approximately 190 x 240 mm (7½ x 9½ in) • cling film • strong tape • textured paper • yellow, orange, blue and lime green acrylic paints • PVA glue • needle from your kit • yellow, orange and blue embroidery thread • pencil • ruler • tracing paper • template

1 Draw a rectangle the same size as the orange card, onto the thick card. Cover the thick card with a sheet of cling film, securing it on the back with tape. Make sure that the cling film is pulled taut and is wrinkle-free.

2 Paint small areas of the textured paper with the four paint colours. When the paint is dry, trace out nine flowers and nine flower centres from the template onto the painted areas of the textured paper. Cut out the flowers and place to one side.

3 Spread a thin layer of PVA glue over the marked area of the cling film covered card. Arrange the coloured flowers, right-side up, on the glued area and spread a little more glue over the top of them. Keeping the design flat at all times, place it somewhere warm to dry overnight.

4 When the PVA is completely
dry, it should have a semi-
opaque appearance. Carefully
peel off the decorated PVA
from the cling film.

5 Using the needle and embroidery threads,
sew approximately ten randomly spaced and
coloured French knots following the
instructions on page 11.

6 Lay the decorated PVA
piece on the front of
the greetings card.
With a coordinated
cotton thread, sew the
PVA onto the card,
using a running stitch
all the way round the
end. You can either
sew this by hand or use
a sewing machine.

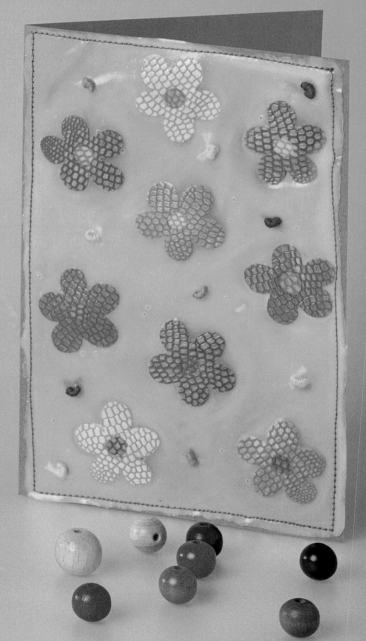

HANDMADE
Envelopes

Give your greetings cards a touch of class by making coordinating envelopes for them. The envelope could be in a matching pattern or colour, or it can simply contain a detail to echo the design of the greetings card.

Equipment and Materials
envelope (for template) • paper • pencil • scissors • craft knife • glue • decoration • length of ribbon

1 Take an envelope big enough to take your card and unstick it. Use this as your template. Place the template on the back of the paper you wish to use and draw round it. Cut round the outline with a pair of scissors.

2   Following the creases on your template, fold and glue the three flaps into position. Crease the top flap of the envelope firmly and fold it into shape. When the card is in the envelope, wrap the ribbon round it and tie a bow above the flap.

FINISHING
Touches

Y ou could take many of the designs in this book a step further and create matching gift tags and wrapping paper to harmonise with your greetings cards. Techniques which would be particularly suitable for the wrapping paper are the stencilling on the baby card, the wooden block printing on the wedding card, the spiral art patterns and the wax resist. For the gift cards, repeating an element of the design will be sufficient – use a single pressed flower or one of the designs from the wire card, or make a border to match one of the printed cards.

GIFT TAGS

Depending on your design, your gift card can be flat or folded. You can make a simple envelope for it, following the instructions for the handmade envelope on pages 44–45, or you can punch a hole in the top and thread through a small length of ribbon or string.

1 Using a craft knife and ruler, cut a small piece of card approximately 50 x 70 mm (2 x 3 in). For a folded card, simply double the width. Apply the design of your choice to the outside.

2 Using a small hole punch, make a hole in the top left-hand corner of the card and use ribbon or string to tie the tag to the gift.

WRAPPING PAPER

Use a lightweight paper that is easy to wrap round your gift. The choice is endless – tissue paper, sugar paper, brown paper or even wallpaper. Use one of the printing techniques for the paper, perhaps choosing a different colour from the card for contrast. Try using a gold or silver pen on dark paper – the effect is stunning.

1 Two layers of paper is very effective. When you have designed your first sheet of paper, cover it with tracing paper to give a soft and gentle look.

2 Plain brown paper and rough string is a very popular way of wrapping presents. For added interest, you can use coordinating colours to paint a random, abstract pattern.

Conclusion

The projects described in this book have shown you how to use simple, easy to master, but very effective methods so that you can make your own striking and original greetings cards.

If you want to broaden your scope, try out other interesting techniques such as marbling, cut-outs or, for a really special effect, the use of gold leaf. Feel free to experiment with the techniques and designs and, of course, with the many different papers that are available.

As you discover the joy of making your own greetings cards, you will bring enormous pleasure not only to yourself, but also to the people fortunate to receive them.

Paper Collage p.16

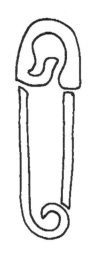

Simple Stencil p.26

Textured Sandpaper p.22

Vibrant PVA p.42

Twisted Wire p.24

Fabric Collage p.34

Luxury Embossed p.28

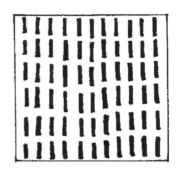

Block Printing p.32

Chinese Dough p.38   Sophisticated Metal p.36